DATE DUE			

GUAM

GUAM

William Lutz

CHELSEA HOUSE

LV15-004087

Library of Congress Cataloging-in-Publication Data

Lutz, William.
   Guam.
   Includes index.
   Summary: Surveys the history, topography, people, and culture of Guam,
with an emphasis on its current economy, industry, and place in the
political world.

   1. Guam. [1. Guam]
   I. Title.
   DU647.L88   1987   996'.7   87-783

   ISBN 1-55546-164-6

Senior Editor: Elizabeth L. Mauro
Associate Editor: Linda Fridy
Chief Copy Editor: Melissa Padovani
Copy Editor: Crystal G. Norris
Art Director: Maureen McCafferty
Production Manager: Brian A. Shulik

Contents

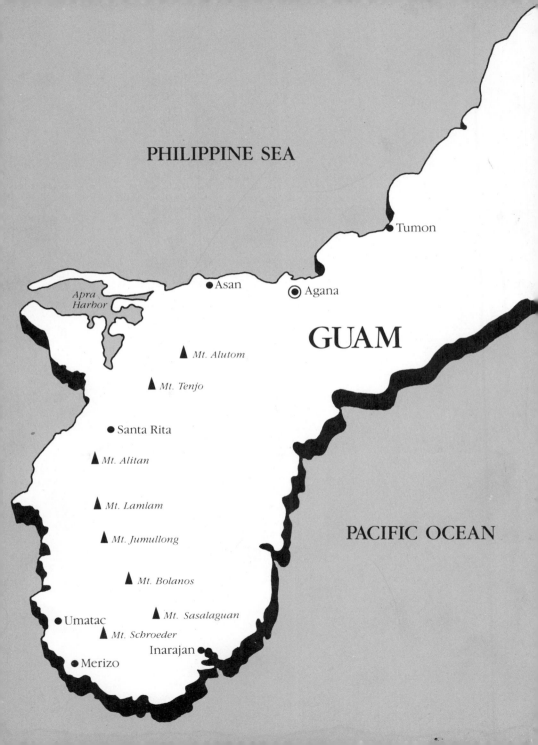

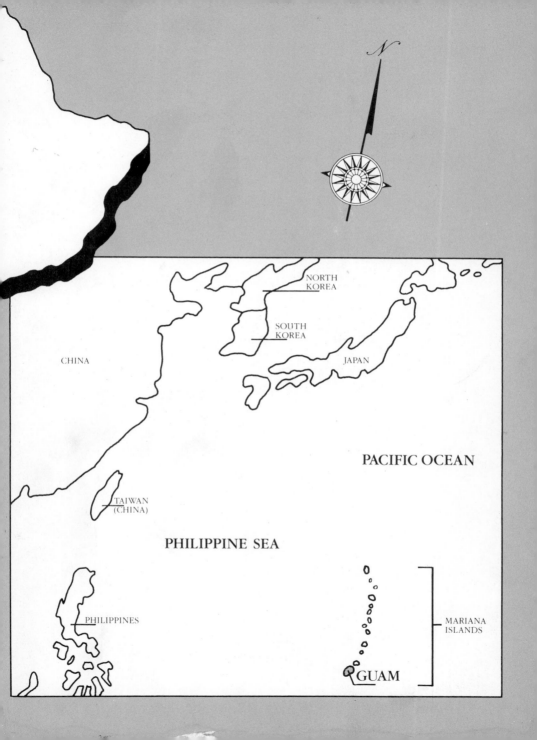

Magellan's historic voyage around the world in 1521 marked the first landing of Europeans on Guam and the beginning of European interest in the Pacific islands

Introducing Guam

Located in the western central part of the Pacific Ocean, the island of Guam is a United States territory. It is the largest and most southerly of the Mariana Islands, an island chain that runs north and south about 1,400 miles (2,240 kilometers) east of the Philippines and Japan. Although its chief importance to the United States is as a military base midway between America and Asia, Guam is also becoming a popular tourist resort.

For centuries, Guam's residents have been the Chamorro people, who came to the Mariana Islands from Indonesia and the Philippines in about 3000 B.C. Portuguese explorer Ferdinand de Magellan was the first European to discover Guam, in 1521, during the first recorded voyage around the world. Spain claimed the island from the 16th century until the end of the 19th century. After Spain lost the Spanish-American War in 1898, Guam became a United States possession. The United States has controlled it ever since, except for several years of Japanese occupation during World War II. American forces recaptured the island after many bitter battles with the Japanese.

The Guamanian people are citizens of the United States, but they cannot vote in national U.S. elections. A governor appointed by the United States president supervises the local government on Guam. One of the important issues facing Guamanians today is whether the island should become independent. Many Guamanians favor changing their island from a territory to a commonwealth to gain greater powers of self-government.

For now, however, it seems likely that the United States will keep this strategically valuable site. Located between Japan, Hawaii, and the Philippines, Guam is America's westernmost possession. Its location makes it an ideal military base, aircraft refueling point, and long-distance communications center.

Lush vegetation, white sand beaches, and clear waters characterize many of Micronesia's islands

Despite its military installations and modern capital, Guam has many of the qualities of a quiet, isolated island: coral reefs, white beaches, balmy breezes, and small villages.

Today, the economy of Guam depends on financial aid from the United States and on large sums of money paid as rent for the U.S. military installations. The Guamanians hope to increase their island's income from tourism and to become less dependent on the military establishments. They also plan to improve Guam's agriculture and fishing industries, in the hope that greater economic self-sufficiency will help them obtain more political independence.

Natives use boats to travel from village to village in the many small islands of Micronesia

Gateway to Micronesia

The island of Guam and the other Mariana Islands are part of Micronesia—a large group of islands, archipelagoes (island chains), and atolls (circular coral reefs) scattered across the central Pacific, mostly north of the equator. Micronesia shares the Pacific with two neighboring island groups: Melanesia and Polynesia. Together, Micronesia, Melanesia, and Polynesia comprise Oceania—a vast expanse of islands spread over an ocean area of about 8 million square miles (20,720,000 square kilometers), covering one-seventh of the earth's surface. Population figures for Oceania are inexact, but officials estimate the total population at about 11 million people. Most of Oceania's inhabitants live on large island groups in Polynesia, such as New Guinea, Hawaii, New Zealand, and Fiji.

Micronesia, which takes its name from the Greek words for "small islands," includes some of the smallest islands in the Pacific. Guam is the largest island in Micronesia, which also includes the Republic of Kiribati, the Republic of Nauru, and the U.S. Trust Territory of the Pacific Islands. The Trust Territory, in turn, includes the Commonwealth of the Northern Marianas, the Federated States of Micronesia, the Republic of Belau, and the Republic of the Marshall Islands.

Because the United States administers much of Micronesia, the U.S. flag flies at all ceremonies

15

Although the total land area of Micronesia is only 1,210 square miles (3,130 square kilometers)—slightly larger than the state of Rhode Island—the island group spans 4,497,595 square miles (11,649,000 sq km) of the Pacific Ocean. Of the hundreds of Micronesian islands, only 125 are inhabited. Their total population is 322,400.

Since Ferdinand de Magellan discovered Guam in 1521, several different countries have ruled Micronesia. Spain was the first country to take possession of the islands. Later, Germany, Japan, the United States, and Great Britain established control over a number of Micronesian islands.

Like Guam, the other Micronesian islands that are currently United States possessions are moving toward self-government. In 1965, the first Congress of Micronesia met on the island of Saipan. After a series of meetings over the next 13 years, the Congress signed a "Statement of Agreed Principles for Free Association" on April 9, 1978, in Hilo, Hawaii. This agreement outlined the procedure to be followed in moving toward independence. On July 12, 1978, voters on all the islands were asked to decide their political future. Voters in the Marshalls and Belau decided to form political districts of their own. The districts of Yap, Kosrae, Pohnpei, and Truk joined to form the Federated States of Micronesia. Thus, three separate island nations were organized: the Republic of the Marshall Islands, the Republic of Belau, and the Federated States of Micronesia.

Under their agreement with the United States, these new countries have 15 to 30 years to gain full control over their internal and external affairs. During this time, they will continue in free association with the United States. In exchange for the right to use the islands as military bases, the United States will provide financial support for the islands to build a self-supporting economy.

Eventually, the Federated States, the Marshall Islands, and Belau will become independent. The Northern Marianas will have their own local government, but they will remain a United States territory and their people will become U.S. citizens. The political development of Micronesia still has a long way to go, but the process has finally begun. For the first time in almost 500 years of foreign domination, the islanders have a chance to become truly independent.

One of the major problems facing Micronesia today is providing adequate medical care for its people. Epidemics of cholera and tuberculosis frequently sweep through the islands, and leprosy is common on some of them. Poor public water and sewage systems help spread disease. The government has built some hospitals and medical clinics, but much more must be done to improve general health care.

The future of Micronesia depends on many things. The island nations have embarked on a political course that will soon lead to independence. They face serious challenges in building self-supporting economies and improving the quality of health care. Yet the people of Micronesia have confidence in themselves, in their new political systems, and in their ability to build their small nations into prosperous homelands.

Each year, Guam's beaches attract thousands of tourists

The Territory of Guam

Guam lies at the southern end of Micronesia's Mariana island chain. The island's name comes from the native Chamorro word *guahan*, which means "we have." It is 30 miles (48 kilometers) long and 4 to 8 miles (6 to 13 km) wide. With an area of 209 square miles (541 square kilometers), it is the largest island in Micronesia.

Guam has two geographic regions: a limestone plateau in the north, and volcanic hills in the south. Covered with thick jungle, the plateau has an overall elevation of 500 feet (150 meters) bordered by 575-foot (175-m) cliffs along the coast. The volcanic ridge of hills in the south reaches 1,332 feet (406 m) at Mt. Lamlam. Other high points in this region include Mt. Jumullong Manglo, at 1,086 feet (331 m); Mt. Bolanos, at 1,220 feet (372 m); and Mt. Sasalaguan, at 1,109 feet (338 m).

Guam has a tropical climate. Temperatures range from 70° to 90° Fahrenheit (20° to 32° Centigrade). Two-thirds of the average annual rainfall of 95 inches (2,400 millimeters) falls between July and November. The dry season extends from January through April. Between 1948 and 1977, about 80 typhoons passed within 186 miles (300 kilometers) of the island and caused more than $1 billion worth of damage. Since the 1800s, Guam has had 16 earthquakes.

19

Guam is an island of diverse sights. Its interior boasts spectacular, crashing waterfalls, as well as seldom-visited jungles. The U.S. military base covers most of the northern part of the island. On the northern coast lies Tumon Bay, a plush resort area popular with tourists. Nearby lies Agana, Guam's capital city and major business district. The island's central region forms a residential area for military families. Lake Fena, in the southern part of the island, is the largest lake in Micronesia. It is now a restricted area where the

The island's hilly terrain offers many views of the surrounding Pacific Ocean

navy stores ammunition and missiles. Along the southern coast, the quiet villages of Umatac, Merizo, and Inarajan speak of Guam's past.

The warm, clear waters off the coast of Guam are the island's major tourist attraction. Water temperature averages 80° Fahrenheit (26.6° Centigrade), with visibility of 100 to 200 feet (30 to 60 meters). The calm waters off the island's western beaches are perfect for swimming, sunbathing, boating, fishing, and exploring. The eastern beaches boast high waves that draw surfers from all over the

Guamanian women weave baskets and mats from coconut palm fronds

world. The beach by Talofofo Bay is especially good for surfing because there are no reefs to break the waves.

Plant and Animal Life

After World War II, United States military airplanes flew over Guam and dropped seeds for *tangantangan,* a rapidly growing ground cover. It was planted to prevent soil erosion, because almost all the vegetation on the island had been destroyed during the long battle to capture it from the Japanese. The tangantangan now covers most of the northern part of Guam in almost impenetrable thickets. However, the plant did not take root in the volcanic soil on the southern part of the island.

Guam's symbol is the scarlet-blooming bougainvillea. This and other tropical flowers—such as hibiscus, plumeria, and flame tree—grow abundantly on Guam, especially in the jungle of the interior. The popcorn bush, ixorasp, rose, marigold, canna, peacock flower, jatropha, and vinca are other flowering plants commonly found on the island.

The Pineapple Plantation, at Yigo in the northeastern part of the island, sports acres of breadfruit, soursop, mango, and papaya trees. On the southern shore, the Inarajan Shore Botanical Garden has rare varieties of tropical flowers, palm trees, and birds—all in a tranquil, seaside setting. At Agat, on the western side of the island, is the Namo Falls Botanical Gardens. Here, in a rustic atmosphere, visitors can swim in the Namo River and splash in the Namo Falls, surrounded by luxuriant tropical plants and flowers.

The most important plant on the island is the coconut tree. For centuries, it has provided the natives with milk, coconut meat, and leaves for weaving cloth and thatching roofs. Today, islanders have found even more uses for this tree. The dried meat of the coconut, called copra, is used to make coconut oil, which is the raw material for margarine, soap, candles, and many cosmetics and suntan lotions. The meat is also used in baking and making candy.

The colorful Marianas fruit dove is the territorial bird

The sweet milk can be drunk right from the nut. The inside rind is used to make brushes, mats, and rope. The hollowed husk can be used for cups, dishes, and ornaments. The leaves are used in baskets, mats, roofs for houses, and even clothes. To the Guamanian, the coconut tree represents life.

When the Japanese occupied the island during World War II, they introduced the giant African snail as a wartime survival food. Today, this snail is a pest and a scavenger, destroying plants and crops. With few natural enemies on the island to control its numbers, the snail population continues to grow and damage the vegetation.

The Guam rail, or koko, is a flightless bird found only on Guam. However, it and many other Guamanian birds are in danger of extinction. In 1946, a United States Navy ship accidentally brought a brown, tree-climbing snake from the Philippines to Guam. This snake climbs trees to feed on birds and bird eggs and has all but eliminated the native bird population from the southern part of the island. The bridled white-eye is already extinct. If the present rate of extinction continues, Guam may be one of the first places on earth to lose all of its native birds.

The coral reefs around Guam are home to one of the most diverse marine-life populations in the world. More than 300 species of coral populate the reefs. The coral formations provide a shelter for algae, plankton, and other small plants that attract more than 800 species of fish and shellfish, including parrot fish, pearl shells, and crab. Two endangered species of sea turtles—the green turtle and the hawksbill turtle—are also found in the waters around Guam.

The waters surrounding Guam provide a habitat for a variety of marine life, including turtles such as this one. These creatures, now endangered, can live to be more than 100 years old

Agana and Other Cities

Guam is a blend of modern-day influences and the romantic, South Sea Islands lifestyle of centuries past. Agana is a modern city—

complete with traffic jams at rush hour along Marine Drive, fast-food restaurants, and air-conditioned shopping malls. But hiking trails in the island's dense, jungle interior lead to hidden waterfalls and swimming holes. And the island's coastline boasts numerous ruins dating from the first Spanish settlers as well as from the ancient people who settled the island almost 5,000 years ago.

Founded in 1668, Agana is the oldest European city in the Pacific and is fast becoming the commercial center of the western Pacific. Several international banks and corporations have established offices in Agana to take advantage of Guam's strategic posi-

26

Present-day Agana serves as the capital of the territory and is a major commercial center

tion. Factories there can assemble goods and ship them throughout the Pacific and Asia.

In addition to Agana, Guam has 20 other towns. Most of them are small villages of 1,000 to 2,000 people. They include Agana Heights, Yigo, Talofofo, Merizo, Umatac, Agat, Santa Rita, Asan, Tamuning, and Toto.

In 1962, a typhoon destroyed nearly 90 percent of the buildings on Guam. Since then, most of the buildings have been rebuilt of concrete and brick, ushering in the era of modernity that characterizes Guam today.

Latte, *stone pillars used in ancient times to support the homes of wealthy Chamorros, still stand in parts of the island*

History of an Island

Guam's first settlers were people from Southeast Asia and Malaya who traveled from the Malay Peninsula to the Philippines and then to Guam in about 3000 B.C. By 800 A.D. these people had developed a complex society throughout the Marianas.

In Guam, the native inhabitants called themselves the Chamorro. Today, the most common relics of ancient Chamorro society are the *latte*, large, stone pillars once used to support the homes of the *matua*, or upper class. The latte are found in double rows of 6 to 14 stones. Each stone is several yards (meters) tall and is composed of a *haligi* (pedestal) and a *tasa* (cap). The tasa is a natural, coral formation placed on top of the haligi with its curved side down, so that the stone pillar looks like a giant mushroom with its top inverted. Carvings on these stones seem to reflect local designs. Ancient burial grounds are often found nearby.

The Western world became aware of Guam in 1521, when the first Europeans, Spaniards under the command of Portuguese explorer Ferdinand de Magellan, arrived. King Charles I of Spain had employed Magellan to sail around the southern tip of South America and then westward across the Pacific Ocean. Magellan did not find the main island groups of Oceania, but he did discover Guam,

Although the Chamorros saved his crew, Magellan misunderstood native customs and ordered his men to burn Chamorro homes

as well as one of the Tuamotu Islands in the eastern part of Polynesia. This voyage was the beginning of European interest in exploring, colonizing, and trading with the islands of the Pacific.

Setting sail on September 20, 1519, from San Lucar de Barrameda, Spain, Magellan sailed around the tip of South America through the straits that now bear his name. He lost two of his five ships there. Then, he and his surviving crew sailed across the Pacific Ocean, amazed at this wilderness of water newly discovered by Spanish explorer Vasco Núñez de Balboa.

For three-and-one-half months, Magellan sailed across the Pacific without sighting land. Unable to renew their provisions, he and his men were forced to live on their rapidly deteriorating food and water supplies. Antonio Pigafetta, the chronicler of Magellan's journey, wrote of how worms reduced the biscuits to powder and of how the crew had to hold their noses when they drank the putrid water. Leather from the ships' rigging was dragged overboard and left for four days to soften in the seawater—and then it was eaten. The crew ate sawdust and any rats it could find.

Finally, Magellan sighted land in the vicinity of Guam on January 24, 1521. Eleven days later, he saw natives in outrigger canoes. They meant salvation. Magellan landed at Umatac Bay, where the natives welcomed him and his starving, diseased crew with fresh water and food. The Chamorro custom of hospitality dictated that as hosts, the natives were to provide Magellan with whatever he needed. But native custom also established that as a guest, Magellan had to give gifts in return. So the natives climbed aboard Magellan's ships and helped themselves to whatever articles caught their fancy.

Magellan opened the Micronesian islands to exploration

Chamorros paddling canoes greeted Magellan's ships

Magellan and his crew did not know that what the natives were doing was their custom. To the Europeans, they were simply thieves. One of the items the natives took was Magellan's skiff (small rowboat), and he was determined to get it back.

Magellan took 40 of his men ashore, burned 50 native houses and boats, killed 7 native men, and took his skiff back to his ship. After returning to his ship and replenishing his supplies, Magellan sailed away to the Philippines. He named Guam "Isla de los Ladrones," or "Island of Thieves." A little less than two months later, he was killed in a fight with natives on the Philippine island of Mactan.

Magellan's historian described the people of Guam as "tall and robust, not too dark with skin pigmentation somewhere between that of the American Indian and the Oriental. The men were handsome and powerfully built and the women were unusually opulent, corpulent busted, and graceful." The natives, he observed, were a "carefree, laughing people, fond of festive dancing and singing, of storytelling, and legend-spinning." This idyllic life, however, ended with the arrival of Spanish settlers.

In 1565, Miguel López de Legaspi, who had led the colonization of the Philippines, claimed Guam for Spain. Spain did not, however, establish a colony immediately. In 1668, Jesuit missionaries arrived to preach to the natives and to convert them to Christianity. Together with a force of Spanish soldiers, they set up the first permanent base and Christian mission on Guam. The missionaries were unsuccessful in converting the Chamorros, who resented the Spaniards' efforts to wipe out their native customs. The natives rose in revolt against the Spanish colonizers in 1670.

Under the command of Captain José de Quiroga, the Spanish troops waged a 15-year war of extermination against the Chamorros. The natives' spears were not very effective against Spanish gunpowder. In addition, smallpox and influenza epidemics broke out among the natives. The bloody war, combined with the diseases, almost wiped out the Chamorro population. On top of everything else, violent typhoons struck the island in 1671 and 1693, killing many people and causing great destruction. By 1741, fewer than 5,000 Chamorros survived, compared to the 80,000 who had lived on Guam in 1668.

Umatac Bay provided a haven for Magellan and his crew

The survivors of those terrible times were mostly women and small children. The Spaniards relocated them to controlled settlements, where the women eventually married Spanish and Filipino soldiers and adopted their cultures and religions. These mixed families are the ancestors of the Guamanian natives today. Almost no pure-blooded Chamorros remain.

In the 17th century, Guam became an important port for Spanish galleons sailing between Mexico and the Philippines. It took three months to sail ~~east~~ west from Mexico to Manila—and six months to return, because the winds and currents move in an easterly direction. Guam was a welcome port at which to break the long journey. Occasionally, galleons sailing from Spain to Manila also stopped for supplies. *from the east to the west*

34

Guam lost its importance to the Spanish empire when Mexico won its independence in 1821 and the Spanish trade in the Pacific ended. There were no natural resources on the island worth exploiting, and neither Spain nor the rest of the world seemed concerned about the island's future.

On June 20, 1898, the United States warship *Charleston* entered Apra Harbor near Agana, firing her guns as she came. The Spanish governor was embarrassed and sent a message to the cap-

In the 17th century, Spanish galleons frequently stopped at Guam on their trips from Mexico to Manila

Agana remained a quiet village until the world wars made Guam strategically important

tain of the American ship, saying that he could not return the salute because he was out of gunpowder. When he was told that Spain and the United States were at war, the governor promptly surrendered. Later that year, the United States won the Spanish-American War and received Guam as part of the settlement. Germany took over the remaining Mariana Islands and all other Spanish possessions in Micronesia.

From 1898 to 1941, the United States Navy administered Guam as a military base, governing everyone who lived there—natives, American civilians, and soldiers. A series of naval officers appointed by U.S. presidents served as governors of the island. U.S. Marines served as the police, and law consisted of general proclamations issued by the commanding office. There was no trial by jury.

Meanwhile, the other Mariana Islands were the objects of a power struggle involving Germany, the United States, and Japan. During World War I, Japan occupied all of the Marianas except Guam. When the Allies defeated Germany in 1918, Japan received control of the German possessions in Micronesia under a League of Nations mandate. Agreeing not to establish fortifications or military and naval bases on any of the islands, Japan took over the Northern Marianas, the Carolines, and the Marshalls.

In 1922, the United States and Japan signed a treaty guaranteeing that Micronesia would remain neutral and would not be used for military purposes. In 1935, however, Japan withdrew from the League of Nations and promptly began building large military bases on some of its Micronesian islands. Finally, Japan declared all of its possessions in Micronesia part of the Japanese empire.

American troops arrived on Guam to displace the Japanese

Japan then began to colonize its possessions with large numbers of Japanese citizens. By 1940, almost 85,000 Japanese lived in Micronesia. Koreans also came to the islands, as laborers. The Japanese built sugar mills in the Marianas and developed bauxite and phosphate mining on Belau. They also developed commercial fishing and large-scale agriculture. None of this economic development benefited the natives of the islands. The Japanese were concerned with their own financial gain, and they did not feel a responsibility to help the natives build their economy.

The United States did not fortify Guam for fear of provoking Japan. When World War II spread to the Pacific, Guam was the first American possession to be captured by the Japanese, on December 10, 1941. Lacking heavy weaponry, the Americans surrendered when the Japanese invaders arrived. Japan quickly concentrated its economic and military activities on Guam and the other Marianas: Saipan and Yap.

On July 15, 1944, United States forces invaded Saipan. Six days later, they landed on Guam at Agat and Asan, on the southwestern shore. The battle for the Marianas was long and bitter. The Japanese defenders on Guam realized that if the United States captured the island it could use its airfields to launch bombing raids against Japan. The Japanese soldiers saw themselves as defending their homeland, and they fought fanatically and to the death.

The first American landings on the island were difficult. The troops met strong Japanese fire. After five days of fierce fighting, the American forces had moved far enough inland to secure their landing points. On July 26, however, the Japanese delivered a strong counterattack against both of the landing areas. This assault, known as a *banzai* after the word the Japanese soldiers shouted as they attacked, was a major setback for the American forces.

American troops fought desperately to prevent the Japanese from breaking through their lines, but some Japanese did get through. So desperate was the fighting that troops in the rear who had never seen battle—including cooks, hospital personnel, radio operators, clerks, and truck drivers—found themselves in hand-to-hand combat with Japanese soldiers.

By early the next day, it was clear that the attack was over. The Americans had not only fought off their attackers—they had killed every one. They counted more than 3,500 dead Japanese soldiers. But the victory was not without a price. American forces suffered serious casualties of their own. Some units lost more than half of

(Continued on page 49.)

Today, Guam's lush, rolling hills show few signs of the fierce battles that raged there during World War II

Agana, Guam's modern capital, grew along the shores of a bay

A manamko (elderly person) grinds palm nuts into flour on a stone board, called a metate

Umatac Bay, where Magellan and his crew landed, is now a bustling village

43

Much of Guam's architecture reflects Spanish influences

Roman Catholic churches are found in most villages

The ruins of a watchtower stand at Fort Soledad

An arched gate surrounds the ruins of an old Spanish castle

Chamorro children use many methods to keep cool in Guam's tropical climate

At Inarajan, offshore coral formations encircle a natural swimming pool

46

Board sailors can take advantage of Guam's waves and breezes

Guamanians hope to preserve the beauty of the historic Umatac shore area

Hidden coves and lagoons abound in the Micronesian islands

(Continued from page 40.)

their men. One marine division reported almost 850 men killed, wounded, or missing. And the Japanese still had a strong force to defend the island.

After three weeks of fighting, the Americans declared that Guam had been secured. Of the Japanese garrison of 17,000, only 1,250 were captured. The rest were killed. American casualties numbered 2,124 dead and 5,250 wounded. Agana had been destroyed in the fighting, and other damage from artillery shells was widespread.

Even after Guam had been declared secured, the fighting continued. Some Japanese soldiers fled to the dense jungles on the island and continued to strike at American troops for the remainder of the war. The endurance and loyalty of these isolated remnants of the Japanese army were legendary. On January 24, 1972, Sergeant

Allied troops captured Japanese soldiers who survived the battle for Guam

At the Merizo Memorial Cemetery, Guamanians can visit the gravesites of relatives and others killed during World War II

Shoichi Yokoi was persuaded to surrender to the United States. He had been hiding in a cave in the jungle since 1944. He did not know the war had been over for almost 30 years.

After it captured Guam, the United States quickly converted the island into a supply base for American forces in the Pacific. Guam also became the base of the Pacific fleet of the United States Navy. American forces built two airfields for B-29 bombers and began a bombing campaign against Japan. While building the installations, the forces dredged harbors, built roads and railroads, improved water and sewer facilities, and modernized the entire island. Guam still benefits from these improvements today. To honor the Guamanians who died during the war, the Americans built Massacre Memorial, in the village of Merizo on the south coast.

In 1947, the United Nations granted the former Japanese possessions in Micronesia to the United States as a strategic trust territory. This made the United States responsible for the territories and gave it the right to establish military bases and conduct nuclear tests in the area.

In 1950, President Harry S. Truman signed the Organic Act of Guam, which made Guam a United States Territory. The Department of the Interior assumed control of the island and a civilian governor was appointed. The people on Guam became U.S. citizens and started to pay taxes.

In 1954, the air force established Andersen Air Force Base on the northern end of the island and made Guam its Pacific head-

In 1954, Truman signed the bill that made Guam a United States territory

quarters. Today, Guam is a major military base, and the armed forces own one-third of the island. Military facilities include a nuclear submarine base and a large ship-repair yard at Apra Harbor. During the Vietnam War, B-52s from Guam carried out bombing raids on Vietnam. In April 1975, after the Communist victory in South Vietnam, nearly 100,000 Vietnamese refugees were temporarily housed on Guam.

Today, Guam is attempting to become a major economic force in the Pacific. With an income of $750 million from the U.S. military each year for the use of its bases, the island has a solid economic foundation on which to build its future.

The People of Guam

The natives of Guam are called Chamorros. The word comes from "Chamorri," or "Chanioli," the ancient title of their chief. The Chamorros are descended from the settlers who came to Guam almost 5,000 years ago from Malaysia and the Philippines. Over the centuries, the original Chamorros intermarried with Europeans, Asians, and Americans. Most of the people who are called Chamorros today are descended from the original island inhabitants and the Spanish who ruled the island for three centuries. They make up about 42 percent of Guam's population of 119,540.

The rest of Guam's inhabitants consist of Filipinos (about one-fifth of the population) and small groups of Chinese, Japanese, Koreans, Mexicans, Australians, Africans, Indians, and people from other Micronesian islands. In addition to the permanent population, nearly 21,000 United States military servicepeople and family members live on Guam. It is very much an international island.

It is also very much a Roman Catholic island. The Chamorros eventually adopted the Spaniards' religion, and over the centuries Catholicism has become a part of Chamorro life and custom. Eighty percent of all Guamanians are Catholic. Another 16 percent are Protestant. The remainder follow other faiths or are nonreligious.

Before World War II disrupted the island, villages were the main social and economic units. They preserved the customs and traditions of 19th-century Spain that the Chamorros had adopted from their conquerors. The fiesta, or celebration in honor of a patron saint, was the great social and religious event of the year. A fiesta was one of the few occasions when people would travel from village to village. The Japanese occupation, the destruction caused by the war, and the subsequent rebuilding by the Americans seriously disrupted the old customs and traditions. Most Chamorros, however, continue to live in villages. Those who work in Agana or elsewhere commute, usually in car pools. Village houses are usually made of cement blocks or coral bricks.

A Chamorro woman uses a stone board to demonstrate the traditional method of grinding palm nuts into flour

Although few pure-blooded Chamorros survived the era of Spanish domination, most present-day Guamanians exhibit features similar to those of their Chamorro ancestors

56

Guamanians in each of the island's 21 villages still celebrate fiestas in honor of the local patron saint. Because some villages have more than one patron saint, there are 32 official village fiestas each year. There are also fiestas celebrating Magellan's landing, Guam's liberation in 1944, Chinese Independence Day, Philippine Independence Day, the Commonwealth of the Northern Marianas Anniversary, local births and marriages, and many other occasions. The biggest fiesta is celebrated everywhere, on December 8th of each year. It honors Our Lady of the Immaculate Conception, the patron saint of the island.

A fiesta usually includes a religious procession through the streets of the village followed by a large feast, music, dancing, a village parade, a baseball game, a coconut husking contest, and many other activities. A typical Chamorro feast consists of roast suckling pig cooked on a spit over an open pit, red rice, a selection of various kinds of cooked fish, taro, coconut, crabs, pastries, and *tuba,* a coconut wine fermented from sap drawn from a palm sprout. Another favorite Chamorro dish is chicken *kelaguen,* which is prepared with lemon, onions, shredded coconut meat, and a touch of hot sauce. Other dishes include *escabeche* (fried fish with cooked vegetables), *cadon guihan* (fish cooked in its own juices with coconut milk), and *lumpia* (pork, shrimp, and vegetables in a pastry wrapping). *Pancit* (fried noodles), *bonelos aga* (fried bananas), and *bonelos dago* (deep-fried, grated yam served with syrup) are also favorites.

Guamanians wear Western-style clothes, usually shirts and trousers for men and dresses for women and girls. Women rarely

wear shorts or slacks. Traditional island costumes, such as loin-
cloths for men and boys and woven grass shifts for women, are
only worn in tourist hotels for the demonstration of island dances.

Education is compulsory for all children between the ages of
6 and 16. There are 28 public elementary schools, 5 junior high

schools, 2 senior high schools, and a community college. The University of Guam opened in 1952. It is an accredited institution that provides four-year degree programs in many fields, as well as a graduate program. The campus is located on the east coast of the island, 6 miles (10 kilometers) from Agana on the opposite coast.

Although Guam has miles of paved roads, many Guamanians rely on ancient forms of transportation, such as riding water buffalo

Communications and Transportation

A system of international, underwater cable connections enables Guam to communicate with neighboring nations. In addition, Guam has radio communication with other western Pacific islands. The island also boasts seven radio stations, three television stations, and three newspapers.

Although English is the official language of Guam, the Guamanians still speak Chamorro. The language is rhythmic and melodic, with many repeated syllables. Chamorro is not related to other Micronesian languages. Instead, it has its own grammar and vocabulary, including many English, Spanish, and Tagalog (Filipino) words that have entered the language over the years. Chamorro was first written down by Spanish missionaries in the 17th and 18th centuries. It looks similar to Spanish when it is written.

After World War II, Guamanian officials established a Chamorro Language Commission to determine a standard system of spelling Chamorro. The commission introduced a revised spelling, but the new system made the words look so different that people rejected it. The commission tried a second time and again its recommendations were rejected. The controversy over how to spell Chamorro words still rages on the island.

Chamorros are pleased when a visitor attempts to speak a few words of their language. The traditional Chamorro greeting is *Hafa adai,* which sounds very much like "half a day." Translated literally, "Hafa adai" means "what?" but when used as a greeting it means something like, "Hello, how are things going?" If a Chamorro speaker wants to ask, "How are you?" he says, *Hafa tatamanu hao?* Since this phrase is so long, it is usually shortened to "hafa" or "fa." If

Guam's international airport has flights connecting to major cities in the Pacific

the speaker wants to stress something, he simply repeats the last syllable. Thus, *puti,* which means "hurt," becomes *putititi* when something hurts a lot. Similarly, *dikiki* means "little" and *dikikikiki* means "very little."

Several trans-Pacific shipping lines and airlines make regular stops at Guam. The island's principle cargo facilities are located at Apra Harbor. An international airport northeast of Agana serves five

Micronesian villagers prepare to launch a **bilas**, *or slow boat, which they have built by hand*

airlines, which offer flights to all the major islands in the Pacific. Guam is seven hours by air from Honolulu and three to four hours from Tokyo, Manila, Taipei, and Hong Kong. In addition, local airplane flights connect Guam to other Micronesian islands. A well-maintained system of roads connects villages and defense installations, and a modern highway skirts the southern half of the island, but the dense, jungle interior has few roads.

Government and Politics

Guam is an unincorporated, unorganized territory of the United States. "Unincorporated" means that the United States Constitution and certain other laws do not apply on Guam, and "unorganized" means that Guam does not have its own constitution. Since 1950, the United States has governed Guam under the Organic Act. The act made the natives citizens of the United States, but it did not give them the right to vote in national elections. Under the original Organic Act, the president of the United States appointed a governor to rule the island.

In 1968, the Organic Act was amended to allow the Guamanians to elect a governor and lieutenant governor for four-year terms. The first elections were held in 1970. The amendment also permitted citizens over age 18 to vote for 21 members of a Guamanian legislature. The legislators serve two-year terms.

The judicial system starts with the district court of Guam. The president of the United States appoints this court's judge for an eight-year term. The governor appoints the two judges of the superior court of Guam for four-year terms, and the legislature approves them. There are also police, traffic, juvenile, and small claims courts. Islanders may appeal the district court's decisions to the

U.S. Court of Appeals for the Ninth Circuit and to the U.S. Supreme Court.

The island is divided into 19 election districts. An elected local commissioner heads each district, serving for four years. The governor appoints a chief commissioner to serve as liaison between the governor and the districts.

Guam has a large government bureaucracy. Over half the islanders work for the government, and many others work for companies that provide services to the government.

Since 1972, Guam has been allowed to elect one congressional representative to represent Guam in the United States Congress. This representative, however, cannot vote in Congress.

Little remains of Fort Soledad, a Spanish fortress that once guarded Umatac Bay

The populated areas of Guam have modern roads and transportation systems, but the interior remains much as it has for centuries

In 1978, the United States Senate gave Guam the right to adopt a territorial constitution. One year later, 81 percent of the Guamanian voters rejected a proposed constitution because they felt it did not adequately protect the rights of the Chamorros. In 1982, a substantial majority voted in favor of commonwealth rather than statehood status for the island. As a commonwealth, Guam would preserve the right to separate from the United States in the future and it could govern itself more independently. Guam has asked Congress to consider its request for commonwealth status, but no decision has been made.

The political future of Guam is uncertain, but its status must be determined soon. Officials on Guam want to begin vigorous economic development, but until the political situation is clarified, long-range economic planning will not be successful. Tax laws, environmental laws, business laws, and other regulations all depend on whether Guam will become a commonwealth, remain a territory, or perhaps even become a state. Until this uncertainty is resolved, few corporations will want to invest in the island's future.

Guamanian officials hope to encourage a prosperous future by developing the island's fledgling tourist industry

The Economic Future

Since 1898, Guam's economy has been closely linked to the United States military. Before World War II, Guam served as a naval base in the Pacific. The United States Navy used it as a supply center for ships, a communications center, and a refueling stop for planes making the long flight from San Francisco to Manila. The navy made no attempt to engage in any kind of economic development. Guam remained a quiet, out-of-the-way Pacific island.

World War II changed all that. After the United States defeated the Japanese on Guam, the island became the temporary headquarters for the U.S. Pacific fleet. It also became a major base for air raids against Japan and a supply base for all U.S. forces in the western Pacific.

Before the war was over, army and navy construction crews had begun to build airfields, supply depots, camps, and other facilities. They dredged and expanded the harbor at Apra and constructed facilities for handling the biggest ships in the navy. These activities created an economic boom for the natives on the island. The soldiers and sailors had money to spend, and the natives quickly learned to sell them what they wanted. The military also hired many natives to work on construction projects.

This economic activity continued even after the war was over, as the military continued to develop its installations on the island. The Korean War in 1951 also contributed to the economy of the island. When the military had completed all of its construction projects, however, the spending slowed down and so did the economy of the island.

During the Vietnam War, Guam again became a center of military activity. The local economy grew lively because of increased military spending. But the economic upswing came to a halt when the war ended in 1975.

Guamanian leaders now realize that the island cannot continue to depend on military spending for its economic development. Although the United States military spends more than $750 million each year on the island, this income could end overnight if the armed forces decided to leave Guam. The islanders' goal now is to build a solid economic structure based upon something more permanent than military spending.

Today, Guam imports much of its food. The government is encouraging people to develop small farms to grow bananas, corn, and sugarcane and to raise chickens, pigs, cattle, and *carabao* (water buffalo). Officials hope that such farms will produce enough food for the people on the island—eventually, there may even be enough for export. During the 20th century, the Guamanians and other Micronesian peoples have given up fishing in favor of jobs in government offices. Economic planners hope to reverse that trend. Catches are slowly increasing on Guam, and a commercial fishing industry is developing.

The government hopes to reduce the island's reliance on imported food by encouraging Guamanian farming

Guam's chief industry is food processing, which includes producing soft drinks and other manufactured foods. In addition, several other industries have recently been established, including a factory that assembles watches from Swiss-made components, an oil refinery, a brewery, a furniture factory, a cigarette factory, and textile factories. Officials hope to attract other such light industries to the island.

Guam is a free port, which means that goods can be imported to the island and sold without duties (import taxes) as long as they are not used there. Manufacturing parts can be brought to the island, assembled into finished products, and shipped to another country without taxes. Officials hope to use Guam's free port status to encourage more international companies to establish manufacturing plants there.

Tourism

Tourism is the second-most important part of Guam's economy. In 1984, 364,665 tourists visited Guam, making it one of the most popular tourist attractions in the Pacific. Each year, the number of tourists increases. In 1984, tourists contributed more than $221 million to Guam's economy and provided jobs for 5,000 people on the island.

Guam has more than two dozen hotels with more than 3,000 rooms to accommodate visitors. Tourists can travel to the island by five airlines and by cruise ships. The Guam Visitors Bureau vigorously promotes the island, which has become especially popular with Japanese vacationers.

Guam offers tourists a great variety of activities. Agana has all the comforts and conveniences of a major modern city, and the south coast offers the pleasures of a Pacific island paradise. The island has some of the most spectacular coral reefs in the world, as well as many underwater wrecks that scuba divers can explore. Swimming, sailing, boating, snorkeling, jet skiing, waterskiing, and

The warm, Pacific waters surrounding Guam are home to a variety of marine life, including exotic coral formations

surfing are also popular. Guam offers some of the world's best surfing, with dramatic waves and clear beaches.

The interior of the island offers secluded, jungle trails where hikers can find exotic plants and birds, hidden waterfalls, and quiet clearings. Those interested in history can visit Chamorro ruins, Spanish forts, and the sites of battles fought during World War II. Military equipment of all kinds can still be found where it was abandoned and then taken over by the jungle.

Much of Micronesia retains the unspoiled beauty Magellan encountered centuries ago

Many visitors come to Guam to visit the War in the Pacific National Park and Museum, the only park in the United States dedicated entirely to World War II. It is made up of six sites around the island. They contain fortifications, military equipment, the former headquarters of the general commanding the Japanese forces on Guam, and cemeteries. The most unusual of these is the War Dog Cemetery. Here are buried the dogs used by the United States forces to help locate hidden Japanese soldiers.

Despite an economic boost from tourism, Guam's economy still depends on financial aid from the United States. But Guam's location is its greatest asset. The island is ideally situated to capitalize on the growing economic strength of Asian countries and the increase in trade between Asia and the United States. The economic future of the island is in the hands of the politicians. Until Guam's political status is clear, it will not reach its full potential to attain a self-supporting, modern economy.

Glossary

Archipelago A chain of islands that are part of the same undersea mountain formation.

Atoll A coral island consisting of a reef surrounded by a lagoon.

Carabao A type of water buffalo raised by Guamanian farmers.

Chamorro A Guamanian who is descended from the Malaysian and Filipino settlers who came to Guam 5,000 years ago. Also, the language spoken by most Guamanians.

Fiesta A celebration to honor the patron saint of a town or other locality.

Galleon A heavy sailing ship used by the Spanish from the 15th to the 18th centuries.

Hafa adai A traditional Chamorro greeting, meaning, "Hello, how are things going?"

"Isla de los Ladrones" The name explorer Ferdinand de Magellan gave to Guam, meaning "Island of Thieves."

Koko A flightless bird found only in Guam. Also called the Guam rail.

Latte Stone pillars used in ancient times to support the homes of wealthy Guamanians.

Mariana Islands	The Pacific island chain that includes Guam.
Matua	The Chamorro word for the upper class of Guamanian society.
Micronesia	A large group of islands, archipelagoes, and atolls scattered across the Pacific.
Oceania	A huge island group, covering one-seventh of the earth's surface, that includes Micronesia, Melanesia, and Polynesia.
Tangantangan	A thick, ground cover vegetation planted by the U.S. military to prevent soil erosion on Guam.
Tuba	A coconut wine, fermented from palm sap, that is popular with Guamanians.

Facts at a Glance

Land and People

Area	209 square miles (541 square kilometers)
Highest Point	Mount Lamlam, 1,332 feet (406 meters)
Population	119,540
Population Density	572 people per square mile (1,407 per sq km)
Population Distribution	Rural, 60.5 percent; urban, 39.5 percent
Capital	Agana (population 2,000)
Other Towns	Agana Heights, Yigo, Talofofo, Merizo, Tamuning
Language	English
Religions	Catholic, 80 percent; Protestant, 16 percent; other, 4 percent
Ethnic Groups	Chamorros, 42 percent; Filipinos, 20 percent; other, 38 percent

Economy

Major Products	Soft drinks and other beverages, watches assembled from Swiss components, petroleum products, furniture, cigarettes, textiles

Imports and Exports	Imports, $610 million; exports, $39.2 million (1983)
Major Resources	Coconuts used to make copra, dried coconut meat
Gross Domestic Product	Revenue from military, 30 percent; tourism, 25 percent; other, 45 percent
Currency	U.S. dollar
Per Capita Income	$6,070 (1983)

Government

Form of Government	Guam is a U.S. territory and elects a delegate to the U.S. House of Representatives every two years
Formal Head of State	President Ronald Reagan (U.S.)
Head of Government	Governor Ricardo Bordallo, Lt. Governor Edward Reyes
Eligibility to Vote	Citizens over age 18 vote for 21 members of the Guam Legislature, but they cannot vote in U.S. presidential elections

History at a Glance

3000 B.C.	Guam's first settlers arrive from the Malay Peninsula.
800 A.D.	Settlers throughout the Mariana Islands develop a complex society.
1521	Ferdinand de Magellan lands at Umatac Bay.
1565	Miguel López de Legaspi claims Guam for Spain.
1668	Jesuit missionaries arrive on Guam to convert Chamorros to Christianity.
1670	Chamorros revolt against Spanish colonizers.
1670 to 1685	Under the command of Captain José de Quiroga, Spanish troops wage a war of extermination against the Chamorros.
1671	A great typhoon strikes Guam, killing many.
1693	A second great typhoon strikes, killing many more and causing extensive destruction.
1821	Mexico wins independence, ending Spanish trade in the Pacific.
1898	United States wins Spanish-American War and receives Guam as part of a settlement. Germany takes possession of other Marianas.

1898 to 1941	U.S. Navy administers Guam.
1918	Allies defeat Germany in World War I. Under a League of Nations mandate, Japan takes control of German possessions in Micronesia.
1922	Japan and the United States sign a treaty guaranteeing that Micronesia will remain neutral and not be used for military purposes.
1935	Japan withdraws from the League of Nations and begins building military bases on some of its Micronesian islands.
1941	Japan takes over Guam.
1944	U.S. forces land on Guam. After a fierce battle causes many casualties on both sides, U.S. forces secure the island.
1947	United Nations gives former Japanese-held possessions to the United States.
1950	President Harry S. Truman signs the Organic Act of Guam, making Guam a U.S. territory. U.S. Department of Interior assumes control of the island and the president appoints a civilian governor. Guamanians become U.S. citizens.
1954	U.S. Air Force establishes Andersen Air Force Base on Guam and makes the island its Pacific headquarters.
1975	100,000 Vietnamese refugees are temporarily housed on Guam following the Communist victory in South Vietnam.
currently	Guamanians hope to increase the island's income from tourism and gradually become independent of the military.

Index